# Everyday Gospel

*Making Disciples where Everyday Life Happens*

A Guided Workspace

Brian Hofmeister

With Justin + Cammie Hronek

# Table of Contents

# Introduction

A few things are certain.

Jesus is the hero. He is the hero of the divine story, the hero of the human story; your hero, mine, your friends' too. Even if your friends in your circle don't fully appreciate that yet, they have a hero. Jesus is the Savior of all people, especially those who believe (1 Timothy 4:10).

Equally sure, is that the hero has handed you a *significant* part in his saving story.

### A Great Commandment

"'Love the Lord your God with all your heart and with all your soul and with all your mind.' This is the first and greatest commandment. And the second is like it: 'Love your neighbor as yourself.'" - Matthew 22:37-39

### A Great Commission

"Go and make disciples of all nations, baptizing them in the name of the Father and of the Son and of the Holy Spirit, and teaching them to obey everything I have commanded you." - Matthew 28:19-20

### A Great Counselor

"You will receive power when the Holy Spirit comes on you; and you will be my witnesses in Jerusalem, and in all Judea and Samaria, and to the ends of the earth." - Acts 1:8

### A Great Confession

"If you declare with your mouth, 'Jesus is Lord,' and believe in your heart that God raised him from the dead, you will be saved." - Romans 10:10

Jesus kept it just that simple. With a great commandment, great commission, and great counselor all wrapped up in a great confession, you now most certainly have a significant part in continuing the divine story - the hero's story - who's still saving the world today.

This modest workbook is intended to walk with you week by week more holistically into such a life with Jesus. We're going to make this so stupidly simple that you could trip-stumble-fall in the right direction and still be a gospel giver to someone around you and become a disciple who makes disciples.

Here's to following Jesus, the hero in everyday life, and everyday relationships.

*–   Brian Hofmeister, Justin + Cammie Hronek*

# How To Read this Book

This is a workbook. More than reading through and learning something, be sure to use the *workspace* and *challenge* to form a response that is uniquely your own to the *gospel*.

Each of these chapters is laid-out for a nine-week experience. However, the later chapters, in particular, may slow you down. Those last chapters take more time to internalize and also take more time for people in your circle to respond to you. It's better to wait on God's timing to settle in than pushing your pace ahead or circling back around later.

## Everyday Connection

Every chapter will start with us connecting the content to three different circles of influence in your everyday life.

Brian will talk about *Neighborhoods and Networks,* Cammie will talk about *Family Connections*, and Justin the *Workplace*. When you think about it, your circle of influence is probably already being exercised in one of those more than the others. Isn't it?

Maybe you are the *Neighbor* that everyone can talk to; you host the cookouts and hangouts, send out that email that people actually read, and love rolling out the welcome wagon for anyone who pulls up with a moving van. Or maybe it's a *Network* of relationships you've picked up along the way that are defined by a common interest, or a shared goal, or you just flat out like spending time together and keep in touch. Whether your most regular relationships are defined by street numbers and mailboxes, or recreation and meetups, there's a special kind of Everyday Gospel application just for you. Brian will speak to that.

Or maybe you are the kind of person who, particularly in the thick of parenting, have settled into a circle of relationships around *Family Connections*. You sit by other parents at your child's sports game or rehearsal and over time turned it into a conversation. Your kid brings home a friend from school for a playdate in first grade, then a sleepover in fifth grade, and by the end of twelfth grade several seem to think they live at your house! Somewhere along the way you decided to meet the parents of the kids that your child chose as friends, and found that you grownups made for pretty good friends as well. You connect as dad to dad, or mom to mom, maybe as couple to couple. Then one day when the kids are out of the house, those friendships you've formed around family connections remain. Again, there is a special kind of Everyday Gospel application around family connections. Cammie will give voice to that.

Finally, Justin will speak to *Workplace* relationships. The average person spends more waking hours at work than at home on any given week and therefore more time with coworkers than even their family! So, if you've been that person who loves the team as much as the task, takes the lunch break just to connect, or have gone so far a to invite a coworker to your birthday party, then you too have a unique application of Everyday Gospel to consider as well.

*Neighborhoods & Networks, Family Connections,* or the *Workplace* – we'll keep relating this book to those three circles of influence. Name yours, and get ready to most specifically apply Everyday Gospel there.

## Group Discussion Option

This isn't a group study, but it can be. For a complementary study of the life of Jesus, I'd encourage group discussions around the following Gospel stories:

Chapter 1 - Mark 6:30-44 Multiply the Moment

Chapter 2 - Mark 2:13-17 Dinner Parties with the Tax Collectors

Chapter 3 - Mark 9:14-32 Places Where Only Prayer Works

Chapter 4 - Mark 10:32-45 The Greatest is the Servant

Chapter 5 - Mark 14:12-26 Communion & Last Supper

Chapter 6 - Mark 5:1-20 Troubled Pasts and Telling New Stories

Chapter 7 - Mark 1:14-20 New Fish for Old Fishermen

## Extras

We'll get you a fresh list of *extras* for each chapter. You'll find them on *The Shape of a Circle* podcast (available on iTunes and Spotify, or everydaydiscipleship.buzzsprout.com). These less-than-five-minute audio segments will help you dig deeper into the topics you want more from.

# Chapter One: Making Meaningful Connections where Everyday Life Happens

## Everyday

Where do I start?

In my *Neighborhood and Networks*, I (Brian) talk about family with Jerry while raking leaves. I connect over local sports with Mike. Finding neighbor Gary at our local election polling place, we wonder out loud together where the world is going. Does that count?

In my *Family Connections*, I (Cammie) get to chat with Lauren while our sons have a playdate, make small talk with another mom while waiting for our daughters in ballet class, and connect with my kids over waffles and smoothies. Does that count?

In my *Workplace*, I (Justin) get to make small talk before and after a meeting, have conversations with co-workers over lunch, and discuss with Jason the future of where we see our careers going. Does any of this count?

All of that matters. Any of that is a start.

*Noticing* the people in front of us *while doing* whatever it is we are doing is the start of helping someone connect to Jesus in everyday life through everyday relationships.

## Gospel

One of my favorite stories in the Bible involves Moses and the burning bush. Just another day doing what he always did - shepherding livestock in the wilderness - when he *noticed* a burning bush *and turned aside* (Exodus 3:2-3). From there, God revealed his glorious next chapter in his Gospel redemptive plan for the world - the freeing of a people who would go on to give us the freedom of Christ - *as well as Moses' part in it.*

I wonder what would have happened if Moses never *noticed?* What if he was too busy in his work or too set in his routine? What if he had no margin to wonder that "today" isn't always "just another day?" *What if?*

I wonder what would have happened if Moses never *turned aside*? It's one thing to notice, and it's another thing to care. What if he was so set in where he spent his time and interests that he had nothing left to spend on a new appearance from God? *What if?*

Shifting now to Jesus, how often do you read about him noticing people who are hurting and sick, self-righteous religious leaders and self-loathing "sinners," tax collectors, fishermen, prostitutes, and beggars? It's hard to find a story of Jesus that doesn't start with him *noticing a person.* And all those stories end with him *turning aside* for that person.

Still today, being a gospel-giver and disciple-maker comes down to *noticing* and *turning aside* for the people he puts in front of you.

*What if?*

## Workspace

Make a list of **places** where you spend the most time.

The part of your yard where you spend the most time?

Family birthday parties?

Playdates and extracurricular activities?

Getting your exercise walking the neighborhood or hitting a gym?

Working next to others?

Recreation interests that captivate you most?

Eating in the lunchroom?

Make a list of **people** you see most often in those places.

Give yourself a list of ideas for getting into closer **proximity** with those people in those places. Maybe in your *Neighborhood* it's lingering at the mailbox or being more intentional about noticing others when you walk the dog? In your *Family Connections,* perhaps it's intentionally putting your lawn chair next to another parent at your child's game or putting your phone down while waiting for the line at practice pickup. In your *Workplace,* maybe every Friday you bring the donuts, or every Monday you're the one saying, "Tell me about your weekend?" Make your list here of how you could increase proximity with those in your circle.

Is there a **problem** you've noticed in these places and people that keeps sticking to your heart?

## Challenge

Get your faith and prayers fired up, and then *notice* someone in someplace. The fun part is that you can't plan it or preconceive it. It might be someone you'd expect or someone you never would have thought of. God will either put them in your path or put them on your heart. When he does, your challenge is to 1) *notice* and 2) *turn aside*. Then, 3) enter that person's life with your version of a simple "hello, how are you" and finally 4) expect that this is just the start of something new that God is developing. This is how all gospel-giving begins, making a meaningful connection with the people and places where God prompts you.

## Extras

Are you looking for a little more training on this topic? We've got a few less- than-five-minute segments on *The Shape of a Circle* podcast that we've made for you (available on iTunes and Spotify, or everydaydiscipleship.buzzsprout. com). We'll give you a new list of extras in each chapter.

These are just that - *extra* - and completely optional as we take this journey together.

- *08. Everyday Circles 101: Swap Names*
- *09. Outreach Isn't Extra - It's Intentional*
- *39. Putting Yourself Out there When Your Life Already Feels Full*
- *40. The Art of Neighboring*

# Chapter Two: Eating with More Significant Relationships

## Everyday

Who doesn't love food? We all love to eat!!!

A good slice of Creamy Havarti cheese with a Door County wine (yum). Cheeseburgers with the latest microbrew (double yum). Brats and cheese curds (YUMMY!). Any cheese and its pairing! Or whatever else you love. *We-love-to-eat.*

> I (Brian) tend to get off work early on Fridays and get a few hours before the family arrives home. One of my favorite uses of these few hours is to invite someone over from my *Neighborhood and Networks*, to share a pint on my patio, porch, or kitchen table. There's something about slowing down the end of the week with a favorite friend and a favorite brew that I've come to prop up as my favorite pairing of the week.

In my *Family Connections*, I (Cammie) LOVE coffee. I can imagine myself giving up every other type of food/drink, but if you told me I'd have to stop drinking coffee, I'd cry for days. Pair it with a good friend or snuggling my kids, and we've now struck gold! There is something that allows people to open up and be themselves when you sit with them in the quiet warmth of conversation and coffee.

Unless you work at Aurora Health Care, eating cafeteria lunch food (especially the frozen food vending machines) is never as good as a close-by restaurant. In my *Workplace*, I (Justin) enjoy taking some time during lunch away from my desk and inviting a co-worker to the nearby Chinese restaurant. Who could turn down an all-you-can-eat international experience? Who wouldn't want to stop and talk about something besides work?

*Why is it that the food we love and the people we love, pair so perfectly together?* People are an even better pairing than cheese.

# Gospel

When the very first church came together in spectacular fashion, we're told that "They devoted themselves to the apostles' teaching and fellowship, to sharing in meals and to prayer" (Acts 2:42). One of those four is not like the other. Three of them sound super-spiritual, and the other is just part of your three squares for the day. In everyday life and everyday relationships, eating meals is very much a part of Jesus' plan for what gospel giving is among us.

> Gospel = Good News. Our scriptures use "gospel" as the catch-all label for every good thing given the world by who Jesus is, and what he said and did. Get used to what this word means because we're going to use it a lot!

Yes, in the context of what we read, they're definitely including *Communion* in some (all?) of the shared meals. But more than the snack-size communion celebrations we put together on Sunday mornings these days, the early church feasted over communion. Loud laughter, friends getting together, a generous potluck, enjoying sustenance - all this is ultimately a big player of what broke into gospel vitality and made disciples among them.

The same is true for you, your church, and your everyday circle.

Eating together is time together. Time together increases conversation and makes smiles happen. Awkward unfamiliarity is buffered. Basic needs are nourished. Fifteen minutes fly by like it was two, and an hour feels like we just got started. In short, everyday relationships fall into place when you line up eating as your first domino, and the gospel goes on the move from there.

## Workspace

Who in your *workplace* regularly breaks for lunch?

Who in your *family circle* lingers over morning coffee?

Who in your *neighborhood* or *network* might welcome an invite for dinner?

Which friends would also enjoy including others in eating together?

*Families*                          *Groups of Friends*

*Couples*                           *One on One*

What opportunities are unique to Weekdays vs. Weekends?

Condense all your workspace notes into your two best ideas.

#1 Person you will invite to eat with.

#2 Person you will invite to eat with.

## Challenge

Consider your 21 meals this week (and 100 cups of coffee!), and pick two not to eat alone. Take that lunch break with a co-worker. Use your early morning coffee to set an appointment with a friend you haven't caught up with within a while.

Invite another family over for Friday night pizza or pasta at your place.

Get out your phone right now. Message them. Invite them.

When you eat with them, no plan is required; enjoy them! Just experience how life-giving it is to share good eating with growing relationships. As we go forward in the coming weeks, you may be surprised how much gospel goes back to just eating together.

## Extras

Less-than-five-minute podcast episodes on *The Shape of a Circle* (available on iTunes and Spotify, or everydaydiscipleship.buzzsprout.com).

- *41. BBQ in the Neighborhood*
- *42. Lunchtime in the Workplace*
- *43. Coffee (or a Milwaukee Brew) with Family Connections*

# Chapter Three: Listening to their (Real) Story

## Everyday

Do you remember when reality TV first came out? Not that reality TV is really all that real, but you get what I mean. I can imagine those first rogue producers. They were just sitting around thinking of all the sets and scenarios that could be fabricated, and how they'd want actors to respond and so forth, and then <pause> --- <light bulb>--- "Why don't we just record a real response from real people in those same scenarios... real people are entertaining enough!"

And they are. Sit on a mall bench for an hour, and you'll get the best Hollywood has to offer just watching people walk by.

It's more than entertainment. Real people relate to the hopes and hurts of real people. By paying attention to friends and acquaintances that everyday life affords us, we too can enjoy and join the real stories around us.

One of the most significant influences on my (Brian's) *Neighbors and Networks* is Superintendent Dr. Kelly Thompson. I volunteer to join several of the committees she puts together, but my favorite is just the open "Conversations with the Superintendent," she hosts. No agenda. Only a chance to ask and listen. I get to hear her hopes for our school district. If you want to know where our schools (and then kids, and then families, and then everything else in our community) is heading, you'll hear it first by listening to your Superintendent's heart.

I (Cammie) think it is easier to try to fix things instead of fully listening and responding in love in many situations. In *Family Connections*, my friend Caitlin (and my son's friend) has recently opened up about some difficulties in her marriage on the walk home from dropping the kids at school. Listening to her hope for their marriage's health allowed me to understand her better, love her more fully, and give me an open door to our next conversation when I checked in with her.

In my *Workplace*, I (Justin) had a co-worker, Cardinal, that was passed over for a promotion. I just had to ask how he was doing.

He talked about how he had hoped this was the next step in his career plan. It opened up some hurts as well. Listening to him describe the disappointment helped me to understand what his career meant to him. It helped me know him as a real person. I got to understand what was beneath the surface.

## Gospel

Do you realize how odd it is that Jesus listened to people so much? He listened at length to the down and outcast woman at the well. Jesus listens to Nicodemas - the "expert in the law" - who was not such an expert. Jesus listened to Zacchaeus as he rambled in excitement and Peter as he regularly put his foot in his mouth.[1]

You've got to wonder - did Jesus have anything to *learn* by listening? Probably not.

---

[1] John 4, John 3, Luke 19, Matthew 16

Did Jesus have anything to *love* by listening? Absolutely.

Everyone's has something going on inside and something to say about it.

Not everyone has someone in their life who loves them enough to listen.

*Like Jesus*, we love by listening.

*Unlike Jesus*, we've also got some learning to do by listening. Listen especially for what's beneath the surface of your friends. By now, in our gospel giving journey together, you've started a meaningful connection and shared a meal. After all the talk about the weather, sports, and what they did this week, it's now time to try listening particularly for their *hope* and their *hurts*. It's those two, hopes and hurts, that are your open door to listening to what's beneath their surface.

## Workspace

Picture a time you felt heard and listened to. Describe that experience.

In contrast, describe an experience of what it was like not to be listened to.

What advice would you give yourself to make yourself a better listener?

What *hope* or *hurt* do you imagine to be hinted at in these scenarios?

1. At the fence with your neighbor: "I had to put my dog down this week. She just wasn't doing well. I had her for ten years."

2. Last meeting in your network before the holidays: "What am I doing for Thanksgiving? I haven't decided, I guess. My sister invites us over every year. Mom and Dad come too.

I just picture something more than the usual holiday routine."

3. At your child's birthday party, another parent: "I love this birthday party idea. I wish I had the time or money to do something like this."

4. A playdate for your child and his friend a week before school starts: I haven't gotten my school supplies yet. My mom has been working a lot. I hope I don't have to use my old backpack again. The strap is broken.

5. At work, talking with a co-work: "I wanted that promotion, I have been working so hard to get it."

6. During lunch at work, talking: "I have been struggling with work-life balance. I feel like I am always working."

Now go back through those scenarios again and list an appropriate follow-up question that would allow you to follow that hope/hurt further into who they are beneath the surface.

Let's do the same now for your real everyday relationships...

Have any *hurts* been indicated in recent conversations by people in your circle?

Any *hopes*?

Any follow up questions that would let you go further in understanding who they are beneath the surface?

Okay, let's just say that maybe no hope or hurt has naturally presented itself yet. What kind of questions could you more specifically ask, on the usual topics, that would get this conversation going beneath the surface? Circle any favorites below.

### Work Questions

*What made you want to go into this career?*

*If you weren't doing this, what would you be doing?*

*What's the biggest challenge in front of you?*

*Do you like it here?*

*___ years from now, what do you hope you've accomplished?*

*When will you be ready to retire?*

## Relationship Questions

*When will you know you've found "the one?"*

*What do you like about the person you're with? How is that different from your previous relationships?*

*What do you hope for your kids?*

*What makes each kid unique to you?*

*What do you want to see more or less of in your marriage?*

*Do you ever worry about them?*

*What do you wish you could change about them?*

*What do you wish you could change about yourself?*

### Recreation Questions

*What do you do for fun?*

*What makes it fun?*

*What kind of commitment does that take?*

*Is that just for you, or do you love sharing that with others?*

*Do you get to travel as your hobby?*

## Challenge

Get some time with someone(s) in your circle and go beneath the surface by listening well to them. You'll need to come in with some *good questions*. You'll need to look for *hopes and hurts*. You'll need to ask more *follow-up questions* to understand them further through their hopes and hurts.

Remember, not only are you *learning* when you're listening, you're *loving* them too.

Get out your calendar right now, and set an appointment with who, when, and where.

## Extras

Less-than-five-minute podcast episodes on *The Shape of a Circle* (available on iTunes and Spotify, or everydaydiscipleship.buzzsprout.com).

- *05. Cultivating the Fertile Ground of Crisis Moments*
- *06. Crisis: What to Say When There's Nothing to Say*
- *10. Conversational Curiosity*
- *44. Trust Stories from Motherhood*
- *45. Listening Without Judgement*
- *46. Four [Stress-free] Tips to Inviting People into Your Space*

# Chapter Four: Serving Something Good

## Everyday

The first few seconds of everyone's day tends to start with an alarm, the thought that "I didn't get enough sleep," and the worry "I don't have enough time" for everything that needs to get done today.

The baseline for another 24 hours starts so low so early, with each to their own, and on their own.

It just wouldn't take much from one person to improve upon the day of another. Would it?

It's just not that hard to do something good.

> I remember when apartment doors marked off my (Brian's) *Neighborhood*. No front yard to play in or wave from. No smell of someone's grill that invites your curiosity to come over. Nothing but the numbers 1-12 marked on doors. How on earth would anything good ever come to a neighborhood like that?! Cookies. Yep. Cookies aren't calorie friendly or carb friendly, but they

are people-friendly. So armed with a plate of cookies in hand, my toddler and I would make our way around, serving our neighbors with, "Welcome to the apartment!" or "Merry Christmas" or "Just had extras and thought of you."

Are you ever running errands on a random day and hitting up a coffee shop? It would have taken way too long to watch that coffee pot drip slowly before I start my busy day! Many of the other parents in my (Cammie's) *Family Connections* work from home right now. While it's not on my list of errands, I'm stopping at Starbucks or Culver's anyway and can drop them off a coffee or custard to sweeten up their workday. Those friends often feel thought of, appreciated, and loved by a simple gift on their doorstep.

Some days, I can get all my work done during the day with time leftover (it's rare, but it does happen). I can't go home early, and I pray I never become a social media scroller just to pass the time. On those days in my *Workplace*, I (Justin) look around for others who may need a helping hand getting their work done. I can make their life more comfortable and my company more productive. Usually, I try to do it without having to ask if I can help. Taking the time to give a helping hand on other projects is much appreciated by my co-workers.

## Gospel

Jesus is so good! Jesus is good for people before they believe. Jesus is good for people even if they *never* believe.

> *"The Son of Man did not come to be served, but to serve, and to give his life as a ransom for many."*
> *– Jesus in Matthew 20:28*

*Wait*, say that again?

> 1 Timothy 4:10 says he's the "Savior of all people, and *especially* of those who believe."

> The parable of the seeds and soils[2] suggests that the gospel will only take full fruitful root one in four times.

---

[2]   Mark 4, Matthew 13, Luke 8

Throughout Galilee, Jesus taught in their synagogues, proclaiming the good news of the kingdom and healing every disease and sickness among the people.[3]

You see, Jesus didn't barter, "First believe in me, then I'll do something good for you." Jesus healed the hurting, offered living water to the thirsty, and found all sorts of ways to spread grace, mercy, and goodness to people he came in contact with *before* they believed, and e*ven if they never* believed.

> **"So let us not become tired of doing good; for if we do not give up, the time will come when we will reap the harvest."**
> **Paul in Galatians 6:9**

Yes, belief is the end game. Faith is also the means to every other end Jesus and his Gospel intend. We'll get there. But to give the gospel, why not *start* sharing the gospel *the way Jesus began* giving the gospel?

Do good. Give something good. Serve. No prerequisites.

---

[3] Matthew 4:23

## Workspace

Name some ways that the Gospel of Jesus (and the people who've been a gospel-giver to you) has been good before you believed.

Name a time someone did something for you that made you say, "Wow, that was thoughtful!" *What did they do? How did it help? How did it make you feel? Did that gesture make a positive deposit in your relationship lasting beyond the moment?*

After the last chapter's challenge, you probably know a lot about their family, friendships, workplace, and interests. Brainstorm some thoughtful ideas of what *serving something good* could look like for them.

*Thoughtful things
that are Practical*

*Thoughtful things
that are Uncommonly
Generous*

*Thoughtful things
that Empower People*

*Thoughtful things
that are Gospel*

Dial it all in now to the top thing you could do to serve something good now.

- *Offer to watch their kids so they can have a night out?*
- *Offer a listening ear in the middle of a crisis?*
- *Whatever you buy next at the store (food, clothes, tickets, whatever), buy an extra for them with a note, "I was just thinking of you."*
- *Lend a hand with a house project or take another task off their list?*
- *Make a meal or drop off some flowers to brighten their day?*

*Your Serve #1 -*

*Your Serve #2 -*

## Challenge

Challenge: *Serve something good* to a person(s) in your circle this week. It's got to be genuinely no-strings-attached good for them; serve whether they ever choose to believe in Jesus or not. Just serve them.

## Repeat Challenge

Next week we are changing gears. Instead of giving you a new gospel sharing activity directly with your friends, we will spend some chapters seeing, hearing, and articulating the gospel.

---

When he had finished washing their feet, he put on his clothes and returned to his place. "Do you understand what I have done for you?" he asked them. "You call me 'Teacher' and 'Lord,' and rightly so, for that is what I am. Now that I, your Lord and Teacher, have washed your feet, you also should wash one another's feet. I have set you an example that you should do as I have done for you. Very truly I tell you, no servant is greater than his master, nor is a messenger greater than the one who sent him. Now that you know these things, you will be blessed if you do them." - Jesus in John 13:12-17

---

In the meantime, keep repeating with your friends the gospel-giving we have already learned!

Eat - Listen - Serve

Eat - Listen - Serve

Eat - Listen - Serve

Repeat until this becomes a lifestyle. We will work on putting this into words next.

## Extras

Less-than-five-minute podcast episodes on *The Shape of a Circle* (available on iTunes and Spotify, or everydaydiscipleship.buzzsprout.com).

- *47. The Five Love Languages in Your Everyday Circle*
- *48. Gifts: The Power of a Plate of Cookies (Brian and Melissa)*
- *49. Words: The Small Sparks that Light Big Fires*
- *50. Serves: Putting Your Extra to Work*
- *51. Time: Wholly Present but not Swallowed Whole (Empathy)*
- *52. Touches: Why do Girls Hug all the time? (And Why Boys Wish they Could)*

# Chapter Five: Narrating God's Story

## *Everyday*

We all like a good story.

From box office hits to fiction novels, the nightly news to blogs, vlogs, garage podcasts, and yelp reviews; or just asking someone you care about, "How was your day?" - everyone loves eating up good stories several times a day. And in turn, we love playing narrator on the best stories too!

What's a good story you love to retell?

Better than the latest news or that TV series you've been binging, the timeless story of God is tops.

> As an oil painter, my (Brian's) *Network* is full of artists, people whose craft is just the outward expression of their creative take on life and the world around them. My buddy Harold pushes the envelope more than most. In a recent phone call, Harold cast a glorious picture of love, hope, and tolerance in our broken world. I got enthused. I wanted in on

the kind of story he told! Harold knows and respects where my faith is at, and it opened the chance to be the narrator on how God's story is taking us to the exact destination of human freedom he's dreamed of, just with a different plotline. I tell God's story of the *fall to freedom* in the hero Jesus. Harold proposes anthropology's story needing a turn of tolerance. We tell stories back and forth.

In my *Family Connections*, I (Cammie) find myself battling questions from my kids and their friends about confusing things in the world, especially over hot cocoa or a snack after school. As I do with most explanations, I turn to tell stories - kids love stories! Stories of everyday life in Jesus' time to explain how we should respond. Sorties of how Jesus lived. Stories of God's love and redemption. Stories of his compassion. Those are the kind of stories I want all kids reading, hearing, telling. The one where they know they are loved, cherished, and through Jesus, are saved.

The world has become a very me-first type of place, But Jesus was a servant leader. His disciples followed him and listened to his every word, but he didn't expect anything in return. He gave more to them. When no one would step up and wash each other's feet in John 13, Jesus used this to teach about being a servant leader. In my *Workplace*, I (Justin) get to share this story of Jesus. I get to discuss how you do not need to be a manager at your company to be a servant leader. Helping others when they do not expect it, showing people you care about them as a person, not just a co-worker, and making sure others have what they need to succeed are just a few examples.

No story is like God's story.

## Gospel

Here at the half-way point in our gospel-giving journey together, we're going to break from the doing and soak in some storytelling. I'm guessing you could use a week to catch up on some of the gospel giving activities you've been challenged with up until this point too!

Just appreciate the gospel story of Jesus for what it is...

In the beginning, God created the heavens and the earth.

The earth was formless and empty, darkness was over the surface of the deep, and the Spirit of God was hovering over the waters.

And God said, "Let there be light… and dry land… and vegetation… and birds and fish and animals.

> Then God said, "Let us make mankind *in our image, in our likeness.*"

So God created mankind in his image, in the image of God, he created them; male and female, he created them.

And there began the God Dream for the world. That although entirely sufficient, and complete, and content within himself, he chose to make a world… and all that's around it… and in it… and as the centerpiece of it all he made… us.

> Like him.

> > With him.

> > > Having purpose.

> > > > An eternal soul.

A place in walking closely with him.

We were made because we were wanted.

Our existence is inseparably tied to God's love and God's glory.

## FALL

But then we fell. We didn't fall *out* of God's love, but we did fall *away* from God's love.

*Do you understand the difference?*

It doesn't matter how much you love your spouse, or your kids, or whoever - there are times when the actions of one propel the presence of the other.

"Just can't be around you right now."

"Just can't move on – as if nothing happened."

"I just can't."

In any relationship, the actions of one bears relevant to the other, and when the first father and mother of humanity pulled away -

**pulled away** from the perfect love of God

> **pulled away** from their place in baring the image of God

>> **pulled away** from the very one whose image we were made in

**- pulled -**

then the rest of us pulled away with them.

Fallen.

We learn of the world-wide grief humanity put on God's heart at the flood.

We know of the world-wide rebellion of humankind as they construct a tower to defy him.

Not more than a few short eleven chapters into our scriptures, it seems that all is lost. All have *fallen away* from God's Dream.

## FORGIVE

But God's love is greater, and his dream for his glory is bigger. He will make a path of forgiveness. He will bridge the gap from where we fell from his love. Fallen *away* from love - but again - *we never fell out of his love.*

For many pages of the story, God's forgiveness path took the shape of the family Israel. Israel was just a family before it was a nation, and to the first fathers, it was promised: "I will make you into a great nation, and I will bless you... and all peoples on earth will be blessed through you."

So Abraham left the land he had known for a new promised land.

And Jacob wrestled with God, to know the place of his family.

And Joseph preserved their future.

And Moses led them out of slavery.

And Joshua led them into the land.

And Samuel applied the law of the Lord.

And David expressed how people could chase after God's heart.

And all the prophets pointed to how people could return to God's heart.

But don't miss the forest while walking through the trees.

In each of these stories, characters, eras, and chapters of Israel's history, it was an interaction with God and knowledge of who he was, that was giving shape to a gospel of *forgiveness*. Sometimes forgiveness was being shaped by a promise, other times shaped by discipline, many times, it was shaped in the grandness and glory of restoration. Every one of these showed that the loving-kindness of God was still there for all!

But one shape mattered more than all.

Forgiveness was shaped by sacrifice.

Sacrifice shaped forgiveness at the first Passover, and every Passover commemorated year by year after. Sacrifice shaped forgiveness in the temple, on the altar, and at the Day of Atonement. Everything in the tabernacle was sprinkled with blood. As the author of Hebrews ties it all together: "Without the shedding of blood, there is no forgiveness."[4]

It had to be life for a life.

> The only way to bridge the fallen gap between God and another's life was for a third life to stand in the middle and be sacrificed between the two.

---

[4] Hebrews 9:22

Such a life was promised.

And such a life came.

On the night Jesus was betrayed, he took that *same* cup of the Passover but pointed to a *new* sacrifice. His sacrifice. Him. The new sacrifice was his blood shed for you, and his body broken for you.

"I am filling the gap."

"I am the one who bled for you."

"I am your forgiveness." "I am."

## FAITH

When Jesus said IT IS FINISHED on the cross, that's because it was.

Nothing more needs to be said or done for you to be forgiven and for the fall to be reversed with God,

"Everyone who calls on the name of the Lord will be saved."
-Paul in Romans 10:13

your purpose is restored,

the eternity of your soul is preserved,

your love from God and with
God is walked in again,

side by side,

**love is
love,**

**and love is
again,**

even in all your junk,

even with all your baggage,

even all your shame and shortcomings

even if you fall, you'll never fall away from God

The God Dream is coming true.

## FREEDOM

Is where we go from here different at all from where we've been?

Sinners still sin.

Worriers still worry.

A loveless world is still where we live while we wait for a thing called heaven.

Did Jesus leave too soon?

*One thousand eight hundred years of promises that you'd come to earth for mankind, and you're back to heaven 33 years later?*

*So many questions we want to ask you, and we only got three years of your words and deeds, most of which no one captured in writing?*

*All that's been fallen from just after the beginning... Jesus, it doesn't look that fixed yet!*

*All of your dreams to walk in your love with the men and women who are made in your image -- well, plenty of them still don't love you, and all of them could use a scrub in your image for that dream to come true.*

*God, what about your God dream for the world?!*

*Jesus, why did you leave so soon?*

> "The Lord is my shepherd, I lack nothing."
> David in Psalm 23:1

But to all who have turned their ear to their shepherd's voice, they know him to lead and provide, as well as know themselves to lack nothing.

**Justification has** taken place.

"Their sins and lawless acts I will remember no more." - Hebrews 10:17

There is freedom when God makes sure your wrongs will never be held against you.

**Sanctification is** taking place.

"I will put my laws in their hearts, and I will write them on their minds." - Hebrews 10:16

There is freedom when God makes sure you are more right every day.

**Glorification** will take place.

"For by one sacrifice he has made perfect forever those who are being made holy." - Hebrews 10:14

There is freedom when God makes sure what you have in him will last forever.

The result is what Jesus declared: "I have come that they may have life, and have it to the full."[5]

That's freedom.

He's telling you now...

1. I got all the laws down to a *great commandment*.

2. I got everything that's next down to a *great commission*.

3. I'm sending a *great counselor* so you'll have power.

4. I've wrapped all that in when you make a *great confession*: Jesus is Lord.

This is living. Living in God's story.

---

[5] John 10:10

## Workspace

Let's review...

1. All of us **Fall** from God.

2. **Forgiveness** happened only by Jesus' sacrifice.

3. **Faith** is our only part in it.

4. We live fully in **Freedom** from here.

Now it's your turn. You be the narrator of God's story in your way. Tell it in the way your heart most came alive as you heard it.

Fall                                    Faith

Forgiveness                      Freedom

Journal your personal experience of living with these words from Jesus to you.

## Great Commandment

"'Love the Lord your God with all your heart and with all your soul and with all your mind.' This is the first and greatest commandment. And the second is like it: 'Love your neighbor as yourself.'" - Matthew 22:37-39

## Great Commission

"Go and make disciples of all nations, baptizing them in the name of the Father and of the Son and of the Holy Spirit, and teaching them to obey everything I have commanded you." - Matthew 28:19-20

## Great Counselor

"You will receive power when the Holy Spirit comes on you; , and you will be my witnesses in Jerusalem, and in all Judea and Samaria, and to the ends of the earth." - Acts 1:8

## A Great Confession

"If you declare with your mouth, 'Jesus is Lord,' and believe in your heart that God raised him from the dead, you will be saved." - Romans 10:10

## Challenge

Practice narrating God's story several times. Say it out loud. Tell it to your kids, your spouse, someone you're dating - someone you wish you were dating! Let everyone take a turn telling it in your group or Missional Community. Heck, practice telling it to your dog if it'll listen.

In these upcoming weeks, we'll help you match the gospel story to your story and the story of people in your circle, but first, you've got to familiarize yourself with it like the back of your hand just as it is. *Fall - Forgiveness - Faith - Freedom.*

# Extras

Less-than-five-minute podcast episodes on *The Shape of a Circle* (available on iTunes and Spotify, or everydaydiscipleship.buzzsprout.com).

- *53. Four F-Words That Tell the Whole Story of God*
- *54. Fall*
- *55. Forgiveness*
- *56. Faith*
- *57. Freedom*
- *69. Pieces over Presentations*
- *70. The Whole Bible in Five Minutes*
- *13. Conversations that are Gospel*

# Chapter Six: Telling Your Story

## *Everyday*

Have you noticed that every book you read has recommendations from others on the jacket? Everything you buy on Amazon has reviews - hundreds of them. Every restaurant or establishment you enter has a star rating. And in the ever-increasing age of valuation by "likes," the platinum affirmation is when one friend *share* the post of another.

With a slew of products and places and posts to choose from, that one in a million people decide to try for themselves is often the one that a friend *shared* with them. It's what a share is meant for. That your story can become part of someone else's story.

> In my *Neighborhood*, I (Brian) love the Mobil gas station nearest me. I love that a hard-working father and son run it. I love that if one isn't working, the other is, and they've never hired anyone else. I love that they've immigrated from the Middle East and are "making it" here, and talking different,

and dressing different - they're just super refreshing for me in my 97% Caucasian suburb. I love how clean they keep their place. I love that they gave me my coffee for free last Wednesday! Even though it's just gasoline, I still tell all my friends, "You've got to pump your gas there!" And you know what? They do. I've amassed a group-following of Mobil station gas pumpers in my neighborhood.

In my *Family Connections*, I (Cammie) love shopping at local small businesses. The ones that don't even have storefronts. The ones that are often staying at home, mama's just trying to bring in some income too. So when my mother base of friends asked me where I got my earrings, I HAD to share the story behind them and take out my phone, open Instagram and show more pictures, tagging her in the post so they could go back later and order some for herself. A couple of ladies in our group of friends have these earrings and have given them as gifts or referred their friends. My experience with one set of everyday relationships has made me share with the rest of my everyday relationships.

In my *Workplace*, I (Justin) decided to broaden my knowledge by taking a new manufacturing engineering position. That career move allowed me to change my view on how things need to be designed for manufacturing. I take every opportunity to encourage others to take a position outside their comfort zone to challenge the way they think about how things are done. My career experience got me sharing in my everyday work relationships things that could affect their career. And it has! I have seen other co-workers take that advice and change their career path entirely.

## Gospel

Telling your friends something meaningful about Jesus doesn't have to be any more complicated than sharing about something you love.

When Jesus healed a blind man in John's Gospel (Chapter 9), it stirred up no small attention. Neighbors gawked and talked about the boy (now a man) blind from birth who was now running laps around town. Religious authorities, who also carried real judicial authority in that day, were on a hunt for an arrest. After all, the healing took place on the sacred Sabbath. No one had bothered to list healings and miracles on the original Mishna list of don'ts for the Sabbath, but surely amendments could be made.

With no sign of Jesus in sight, the authorities interrogate the once-blind now-seeing man. They ask him for his story. They ask the parents for his story. They want to know what he was like before Jesus showed up, what Jesus did, what happened since. Oddly, not getting information in the direction they want, they ask him the story a second time and even ask point-blank what they're trying to get at: *What can you give us against Jesus? Give us some wrong we can charge him with!*

We have to appreciate that this man never had eyes to read the Torah. He was never included as equal in places of worship where God would have been known. And now here he is, up against the experts, being put on the spot for answers. *Can you imagine?*

Not being able to hold his own with expert thinkers nor desiring a debate with critics, his reply is delivered with spot-on simplicity: "Whether he

[Jesus] is a sinner or not, I don't know. One thing I do know. I was blind, but now I see!"[6]

Just take that in for a minute for yourself.

There will always be someone smarter than you and arguments are rarely productive. The one thing that can always tell some about Jesus that will never be out-smarted and can never be argued is *your story*. Share it. "I recommend Jesus because my life was once like *that*, but now... it's like *this*."

## Workspace

Name something simple that you love. It could be your favorite bakery item and who makes it best. It could be a movie you just watched, a trail you just hiked, a cat food you sniff (when no one is looking), or a vacation you just took. What would come out in your recommendation? What senses would be excited by your description? Would you tell people where to go and what to do to experience the same? Would you explain what about life just wasn't as good before this? Would you blurt out this recommendation the first second you next see your friend, or just wait for it to come up? Write out your *recommendation*.

---

[6] John 9:25

Now play that same recommender role for Jesus. (*Hint*: If you just recommended a bran muffin and it sounds more exciting than Jesus, then we've got a problem!)

What's the last thing you discovered in Jesus that excited you?

How would you say you've experienced Jesus in a tangible, emotional, or practical way this week?

Name a critical time you had Jesus meet you in one of your *hopes*?

Name a critical time you had Jesus meet you in one of your *hurts*?

More broadly speaking, how would you outline your life story in terms of the whole gospel story?

**Fall** (what your life was like before Jesus)

**Forgiveness** (what Jesus did to get you to realize you have a problem and he has the answer)

**Faith** (what your turning moment was)

**Freedom** (how your life is different now in Jesus)

Re-read that outline you just made of your personal gospel story. Who sounds like the hero in the story? If the hero is you in any way (*your* revelation, *your* response, or *your* perseverance), then you need to go back and rewrite the story with Jesus as the hero.

## Challenge

Just like last week, practice telling the story, but this time *your personal story* in the gospel. It could be the story of how the gospel first got a hold of you, or the story of how the gospel got a hold of you this week, or both!

Say it out loud. Tell a spouse and a few friends. Let everyone take a turn telling it in your group or Missional Community. Keep your story to 3-5 minutes. There's a time and place for a more extended version and also a shorter version, but get used to telling your 3-5 minute story as your home base.

Keep your vocabulary consistent to *Fall - Forgiveness - Faith - Freedom*. The more you get used to telling your story and God's story in the same language, the more readily you'll be able to share both interchangeably with people in your circle.

## Extras

Less-than-five-minute podcast episodes on *The Shape of a Circle* (available on iTunes and Spotify, or everydaydiscipleship.buzzsprout.com).

- *58. Crafting Your God Story in Four F-Words*
- *59. Real "My Stories" #1*
- *60. Real "My Stories" #2*
- *61. Real "My Stories" #3*
- *62. Real "My Stories" #4*
- *07. Authenticity is Life or Death*

# Chapter Seven: Relating to Everyone's Story

## *Everyday*

"I can relate."

It's a defining moment for a conversation. It is the intent from the beginning. When a conversation begins, or a story is told, the hope is to find the words that would welcome someone into a part of your life. The unspoken plan is, "I want someone to be able to relate to me." And in turn, you expect that they will offer some of their own words and stories that provide the same. "I can relate."

> When you live in the same *Neighborhood and Networks* long enough, I (Brian) find that layers of overlaps happen. I made a friend on the first-ever Parks and Rec team I signed my kid up for. He's since come to our church. Our kids go to the same school and are on the same teams. I buy sub sandwiches from their family business. He and I got to talking about the small business climate (which is pretty rough at the time of first printing this). I can

relate. Plenty of parts to my job run just like a small business. He tells his story. I could tell mine. But what part of mine? More than deliberating over economic uncertainties, is there anything in my story with Jesus that speaks hope into these uncertainties?

When you start to form relationships with other parents, you start to find that your *Family Connections* quickly ease into this statement of "I can relate." So often, I (Cammie) will text another mom from my son's class, and we will commiserate over homework or the difficulties of dealing with a particular person in a class. While it's easy to sit and complain about said homework or person, how much more can I add to this situation by sharing how similar problems in the past helped to grow or shape me? And how can we relate that to our boys? How does the Gospel of Jesus relate to everyday life stuff like this?

When you go into the same place with the same people every day, relationships are bound to form. In my *Workplace*, my (Justin's) co- workers and I understand the difficulties of communicating within teams or completing a task up against a deadline. It's just the nature of every workplace to not only figure out how to get the job done, but how to also get it done with the people you've been given to work with. My co-worker and I go back and forth relating to these daily struggles, but how can I bring into the conversation how knowing Jesus is right alongside me during these difficulties helps get me through them? How do I give gospel here? What has the gospel first given me?

When I say to you, "I can relate," and you, in turn, say the same to me, there needs to be a seat for God at the table to say, "We can all relate on this one."

## Gospel

Here are some words from Paul and Jesus on how God's story, your story, and everyone else's story become the same story.

> "If you declare with your mouth, 'Jesus is Lord,' and believe in your heart that God

raised him from the dead, you will be saved. As Scripture says, 'Everyone who calls on the name of the Lord will be saved.'" - Romans 10:9,13

"How, then, can they call on the one they have not believed in? And how can they believe in the one of whom they have not heard? And how can they hear without someone preaching to them? And how can anyone preach unless they are sent? As it is written: "How beautiful are the feet of those who bring good news!" - Romans 10:14-15

"Again Jesus said, 'Peace be with you! As the Father has sent me, I am sending you.'" - John 20:21

I think those scriptures say it all as is. To summarize: 1) Believing Jesus is a salvation (life or death) matter. 2) No one (no friends in our circle) will get a chance to believe unless someone lives as "sent" to them. 3) Jesus sends us (just like he was sent).

While this is the time that your reflex-safeguards usually go up *(What if I offend someone? What if the words don't come out well? What will people think of me?)*, pause for a moment to realize something - the person you are speaking with is *your friend.*

They *trust* you.

And rightly so.

You can be trusted, can't you? You care.

You've listened.

They've already trusted you enough to share their hopes and hurts with you. If that's not where the relationship is at, then go back and repeat the challenges of Chapters 1-4 in this workbook until it is! But if some trust is already happening, they will also trust you enough to speak something into their life if you genuinely believe it will relate to them.

Here is what's trustworthy about what you're about to say - *you'll be talking to them about their story.*

You know that something in your gospel story will help.

You're convinced that Jesus' story will radically help.

But it's their story as you've known it and heard it that concerns you.

Their hopes and their hurts have left some open ends to where their story will go next. And now, you are about to offer something to add to those open ends. The gospel story of Jesus, as you've known and lived it as your story, will offer new chapters and alternative endings that they hadn't known were available.

## Workspace

*Gospel = Good News in Jesus.*

Let's go further in the following scenarios from Chapter 3. Explain what *gospel* would be to this moment.

1. At the fence with your neighbor: "I had to put my dog down this week. She just wasn't doing well. I had her for ten years. I feel like I lost my best friend."

2. Last meeting in your network before the holidays: "What am I doing for Thanksgiving?

I haven't decided, I guess. My sister invites us over every year. Mom and Dad come too. I just picture something more than the usual holiday routine. Besides, they've always seen me as one thing. I'm coming around to see myself as another. I just don't want to be in an environment that drags me down from where I'm going."

3. At your child's birthday party, another parent: "I love this birthday party idea. I wish I had the time or money to do something like this."

4. A playdate for your child and his friend a week before school starts: "I haven't gotten my school supplies yet. My mom has been working a lot. I hope I don't have to use my old backpack again. The strap is broken."

5.  At work, talking with a co-work: "I wanted that promotion, I have been working so hard to get it. Growing up my Dad always said to be recognized as the best meant you had to do the best and never come in second."

6.  During lunch at work, talking: "I have been struggling with work-life balance. I feel like I am always working. Honestly, though, that is where I feel more affirmed and more respected - I feel more at home with my work than I do at home!

Now look back over what you just wrote. Did it sound like excellent advice, or did it sound like *gospel*? While you may be able to point to useful and helpful scriptures, lessons, and anecdotes; it's speaking in terms of *Fall-Forgiveness-Faith-Freedom* that will keep Jesus as the hero and the gospel understood.

Write down three scenarios that you've observed in your circle of relationships. What hopes and hurts are being revealed? What would the gospel specifically be to what they are going through?

1.                2.                3.

Finally, pick one of these **transition statements** that would work best for you in speaking the gospel that could and should be said.

> *I was thinking about what you said last time, and it reminded me of a time that...*

> *I was praying about what you said last time, and I think God gave me something he'd want you to hear...*

> *If I had something to say that I believe would make all the difference in changing that for you, would you want to hear it?*

*You know I'm pretty big into Jesus, so could I share his vantage point on what you're going through?*

*Man, that's where faith in Jesus comes in.*

*One time I....*

*You know, Jesus had something to say about things like that...*

*We all fall like that. But I don't think we have to stay down, and I don't think it's on us to pick ourselves up again either. In Jesus, I've known...*

*It sounds like you're talking about forgiveness. That's some of the most potent stuff in relationships. I'm not the best at it, but what I know has made me better at forgiving is connecting again to how Jesus has already forgiven me. Most recently, I...*

*It sounds like you're trying to do it all and just can't. Me too! I guess you could say that's what helped my faith get started and why that faith for me is in Jesus, and nothing else is like him...*

*I've got a couple of stories where I could tell Jesus met me in something just like that. Mind if I tell you?*

## Challenge

Let's put it all together from your workspace. 1) Name one or two (or three) in your circle, and 2) a hope or hurt that the gospel relates to, then 3) a transition

*"The harvest is plentiful, but the workers are few. Ask the Lord of the harvest, therefore, to send out workers into his harvest field." - Jesus in Luke 10:2*

statement you could use, and 4) the day and time you plan to have that conversation.

| Friend's Name | Hope/Hurt/ Gospel | Transition | Day/ Time |
|---|---|---|---|
|  |  |  |  |
|  |  |  |  |
|  |  |  |  |

Now it's just follow-through on sharing these gospel words to who you've listed when you've listed it.

I know this feels wild, but you're ready for it!

Pray this prayer right now: *Father, I'm available. There are some reasons this is hard for me, but I'm more attached to my love for you and my love for my friend than I am to my reservations. I'm going to look for an opportunity to speak. I need you to make that opportunity so clear that I can't miss it. If you give me that opportunity, I promise I'll do my part and open my mouth to speak. I pray that you'll give me the words I need at that moment - something from your story, something from my story with you, something that will give them gospel instead of advice. Here we go... Amen.*

## Extras

Less-than-five-minute podcast episodes on *The Shape of a Circle* (available on iTunes and Spotify, or everydaydiscipleship.buzzsprout.com).

- *11. Conversational Doors that Open to the Gospel*
- *12. Conversational Consistency and What they Trust You to Say Next*
- *63. Gulp. It's time to say Something!*
- *64. Yep. I said Something!*
- *65. Hmm. God already said Something!*

# Chapter Eight: Inviting to a Shared Discipleship Journey

## *Everyday*

Things that can happen alone happen *better* and *more often* when you're together.

You could have bought just one ticket, but that concert is better with someone you know.

You could stick to that small business venture on your own, but you dream bigger when you have a partner.

You could have gone to the gym three times this week on your own, but you were much more likely to do so if you were meeting a friend or trainer.

You may have planned to sit on your couch all weekend and do nothing, but if a friend invited you out, you said yes, because *together* is *better*.

> In my *Neighborhood and Networks*, I (Brian) became good friends with a professional Life Coach. It was fun to pass book recommendations back and forth with a guy like that. Great conversations

resulted - conversations about values, priorities, and how we balance family. I invited him to be part of a church group I was in, a community of other parents from my church who talked about parenting and Jesus, all in the context of supporting each other. He wasn't ready to join our "church," but he was eager and prepared to journey with a handful of other parents in his stage of life, who were exploring Jesus together along the way.

I (Cammie) love to invite other moms in my *Family Connections* to Women's Retreats. It's such a great way to get out of the routines and grow alongside other women in my everyday life. It opens the door to Jesus without feeling the pressure of inviting them to a Sunday service. Often when one or two women are placed on my heart and come to the event, they leave saying, "That is exactly what I needed to hear." I love the conversation that opens from there. I love how it sets up our relationship to grow in more gospel from here.

In my *Workplace*, I (Justin) get to have conversations with co-workers about where we want our careers to go; what our hopes and dreams look like. While others talk about the last book they read or podcast they listened to about career journeys (which don't get me wrong, there are books with great advice), it allows me to discuss the most critical aspect of a career journey - God's plan. We discuss how you'll probably miss what you are made for if you do not include God's plan in your decision. In a world that resonates with the sense that "I was made for more" or "I must be here for a reason," I can see co-workers sparking an interest in journeying further.

## Gospel

Coming off of last chapter's challenge, whether or not you are ready for this chapter's lesson is more about whether your friend is ready! *Did they welcome the conversation when the topic turned toward Jesus and his Gospel?*

*Discipleship begins before outreach is done.*

They didn't have to turn their life over to Jesus in your last conversation. You're just looking for any sign that they'd like to keep moving forward (closer) to Jesus.

Did they *welcome* the gospel conversation?

Would you say they are *seeking* more gospel?

*At some point the conversations need to go from informal and infrequent, toward intentional and regular.*

Way too often, disciples of Jesus have handed their friends the gospel, backed up, and left them to go figure out what to do with it next - *alone*. However, if you follow Jesus and your friend is following (at least tiptoeing toward) Jesus too, doesn't that mean we're all on the same path? Aren't your journey's going to meet anyway? Things that can happen alone happen *better* and *more often* when you're *together*.

Jesus made disciples with three simple words: *Come - Follow - Me*. It's not any more complicated than that for you to be a disciple-maker too. Whatever you're doing and wherever you're going to grow yourself as a disciple - invite them to come and follow along with you. Invite them to go where you go.

Invite them into growing how you grow. If they're *welcoming* and *seeking*, they'll appreciate the invitation to follow you as you follow Jesus.

> **"Follow my example, as I follow the example of Christ. "** - Paul in 1 Corinthians 11:1

## Workspace

This section's workspace is about you as much as it is people in your circle. I'll point out some of the most core discipleship essentials, and then you'll reflect both on your experience with these (as a disciple) and how to invite others in the same (as a disciple-maker).

1.  **Jesus said that the Great Confession of *BELIEF* is our only work.**

    *The work of God is this: to believe in the one he has sent.* - Jesus in John 6:29

    *If you declare with your mouth, "Jesus is Lord," and believe in your heart that God raised him from the dead, you will be saved.* Paul in Romans 10:9

*Repent and be baptized, every one of you, in the name of Jesus Christ for the forgiveness of your sins.* Peter in Acts 2:38

Since Jesus did it all for you, there's nothing left for you to do other than *believe*. He's got a lot of places he's going to go with you and the people you disciple, but it all gets traced back to believing who he is and what he's done.

Who do you believe Jesus is, and what do you believe he's done for you? (*Hint: Fall - Forgiveness - Faith - Freedom*)

**"All Scripture is God-breathed and is useful for teaching, rebuking, correcting and training in righteousness, so that the servant of God may be thoroughly equipped for every good work."**
**- Paul in 2 Timothy 3:16-17**

What shaped your belief in Jesus in the *first place*? What has helped to continue to shape your belief today? (*Friends? Church Involvement? Scripture & Prayer? Father & Holy Spirit? Rhythms & Practices?*)

*Where do you still have honest questions, or maybe even real doubts? That's a fair question here too.*

Are there any ways you struggle in being defined by what you do instead of what Jesus has done for you?

After reflecting on everything that's brought your belief in Jesus to where it is today (and still forming today), what things can you invite your friends to as well?

2. **Jesus said that *LOVE* is our Great Commandment and the *HOLY SPIRIT* is our Great Counselor.**

    **"Therefore, I urge you, brothers and sisters, in view of God's mercy, to offer your bodies as a living sacrifice, holy and pleasing to God—this is your true and proper worship. 2 Do not conform to the pattern of this world, but be transformed by the renewing of your mind. Then you will be able to test and approve what God's will is—his good, pleasing and perfect will."**
    **- Paul in Romans 12:1-2**

    *"Love the Lord your God with all your heart and with all your soul and with all your mind." This is the first and greatest commandment. And the second is like it: "Love your neighbor as yourself."* - Jesus in Matthew 22:37-39

    *You will receive power when the Holy Spirit comes on you; and you will be my witnesses in Jerusalem, and in all Judea and Samaria, and to the ends of the earth. - Jesus in Acts 1:8*

*The fruit of the Spirit is love, joy, peace, patience, kindness, goodness, faithfulness, gentleness, and self-control. - Paul in Galatians 5:22-23*

*I am the vine; you are the branches. If you remain in me and I in you, you will bear much fruit; apart from me, you can do nothing. - Jesus in John 15:5*

Anything that's of Jesus expressed in our everyday lives will look like *love* and be led by the *Holy Spirit*. It just doesn't work any other way.

It's hard to put love and relationships into words but try it. Just like trying to describe your love for a family member, *where would you say your love with God is flourishing right now, and where (if anywhere) does something try to come between you?*

How is your love for God spilling into your love for others right now, and where do you need more help?

What great ways are you experiencing your power and your fruit in the Holy Spirit right now, and what areas are you "still in process?"

Instead of pretending to "have it all together" as a model to your friend, how do you think your friend would respond if you were transparent about those growth spots? How do you think they would react if you *invited* them into being one of your gospel influencers; someone who helps you change?

## 3. Jesus said that MAKING DISCIPLES is our Great Commission.

*Go and make disciples of all nations, baptizing them in the name of the Father and of the Son and of the Holy Spirit, and teaching them to obey everything I have commanded you.* - Jesus in Matthew 28:19-20

Then the righteous will answer him, "Lord, when did we see you hungry and feed you, or thirsty and give you something to drink? When did we see you a stranger and invite you in, or needing clothes and clothe you? When did we see you sick or in prison and go to visit you?"

*The King will reply, "Truly I tell you, whatever you did for one of the least of these brothers and sisters of mine, you did for me."* - Jesus in Matthew 25:37-40

*"Truly I tell you," Jesus replied, "no one who has left home or brothers or sisters or mother or father or children or fields for me and the gospel will fail to receive a hundred*

*times as much in this present age: homes, brothers, sisters, mothers, children, and fields—along with persecutions—and in the age to come eternal life."* - Jesus in Mark 10:29-30

What we get as disciples of Jesus always gets passed to the next person as well. Gospel always needs to *go*.

Where have you been doing gospel-giving and disciple-making relationships in line with the great commission? *What have you been able to celebrate and enjoy? What did you have to be ready for it to cost you?*

Who can you affirm in your circle for taking what they've received in the gospel and then turning around and being a gospel giver to others? *Have they also turned their gospel-giving into disciple-making, or are they stuck?*

Who else is on your heart for you to be a disciple-maker to? Who else is on your friend's heart that they want to help be a disciple-maker to? What would it best look like for all of you to get together in one shared discipleship setting?

## 4. Jesus said we'd have to walk it out with him.

> "Come to me, all you who are weary and burdened, and I will give you rest. Take my yoke upon you and learn from me, for I am gentle and humble in heart, and you will find rest for your souls. For my yoke is easy and my burden is light."
> - Jesus in Matthew 11:28-30

You can't give your friend a long discipleship to-do list. *You just can't.* That's not gospel. Like many good things that can and should be done, the cart will end up before the horse when discipleship is taken on in to-do list terms. It's always a relationship. It's always Jesus you walk with. The rest gets done along the way when you walk with Jesus in close stride.

## Challenge

Invite your friend to join you in the *places you go* and the *things you do* as a disciple of Jesus. List each friend and the specific invite you'll make to them.

As you do so...

> Make sure your invitation is about *discipleship*, not the *places to be* and *things to do*. The former is the point, and the latter is just the tool.
>
> Also, make the invitation about staying on the *journey* with them. Don't just *push* them out of the vehicle! It might sound like you're inviting a friend to a church service, or to read the Bible, or to join your Missional Community or Study Group, or to help with your service project - but you're not. Again, those are the tools. *Your invitation to them is an invitation to join your discipleship journey with Jesus, wherever and with whomever it goes next.*

## Extras

Less-than-five-minute podcast episodes on *The Shape of a Circle* (available on iTunes and Spotify, or everydaydiscipleship.buzzsprout.com).

- *17. An Antidote to Repeating the Same Old Conversations*
- *18. Taking a Discipleship Pulse*
- *24. Shaped by Serving*
- *23. Treat your Disciplines like your Keurig*
- *66. Organic Invitations: How to Invite People into What You're Already Doing*
- *67. Church Invitations: How to Make a Good Invite to Church*
- *68. Reverse Invitations: How to Invite them to something You'd Create for Them*

# Chapter Nine: Grouping a Community of Disciples

*Everyday*

Grouping is just what we do.

Why do historical societies and book clubs get formed, instead of just a person or two reading their books of choice? Why so many

> **"Birds of a feather flock together."**
> - Captain Obvious

youth sports clubs, instead of just playing games at the park? Why political parties, instead of just a list of candidates on a ballot? Why do high schools and colleges list so many *extra*curricular options instead of just sticking to the curricular?

It's because when one person who is into something finds another person who is into the same thing, then *together*, they get to thinking about how many more people like them that could (or more importantly *should*) get into this too. So, they get organized enough to bring people together, around the shared thing they love.

*"I pray also for those who will believe in me through their message, that all of them may be one, Father, just as you are in me and I am in you. Then the world will know that you sent me and have loved them..." - Jesus in John 17:20-21,23*

People do this around hundreds of things, and Jesus is the first and the greatest. So much so that you don't have to leave your old group for a new group of Jesus followers. Jesus groups get formed within your other groups.

My (Brian's) favorite is when a group forms within my *Neighborhood and Networks* alongside a few friends from my church. In college, a few Christians and I made a "group" for anyone in our freshman dorm that wanted to get into Jesus. In our early career years, Melissa and I made a lunch-time "group" of young professionals who wanted to explore Jesus. After buying our first house, we made a "group" of church friends and neighborhood friends that wanted to welcome Jesus into their parenting. Today, we've got a "group" made up of friends we've picked up from cub scouts, youth football, and church. All of us participate in church together now, but for many years, it was just everyday relationships that got "grouped" together in Jesus.

I (Cammie) have always loved inviting EVERYONE to get-togethers, birthday parties, the fourth of July, etc. My family, my church friends, and my friends through my kids were all in one place at one time. My favorite is when I have noticed growth in a friend and invite them to join my small group or church, and they get excited about it and continue to grow and flourish in that setting. We continually invited my husband's aunt and uncle to church for special events, and they showed up for a random Sunday in October. My kids talk about our kids' program enough that their friends want to start coming too. This kind of "let's do it all together" discipleship is where the fun is! I just really can't picture another way.

In my *Workplace*, I (Justin) get the opportunity to work with different groups of people throughout my career. By growing close to a group of people, I get to know what excites them about life. When it comes to getting to know me, I make sure they understand my love of Jesus and all he does for me. It doesn't have to be forced or sound like I'm preaching from a platform. I've found that giving Jesus credit with others when things go right, or expressing the solidarity I still find in him when things aren't going right - that kind of stuff makes them wonder more about Jesus and how he can help them in their careers and every other part of everyday life.

## Gospel

The power of the gospel is found in many sizes of groupings. Jesus called 1 disciple at a time and then grouped them as "The 12." 120 gathered in prayer after Jesus' death, and 3,000 were "added to their number" (their community, not their bookkeeping) after Jesus's ascension and the Holy Spirit's Pentecost. I'd say that the 1-12-120-3000 approximates the layout of what we have in Jesus as a friend-group-church-kingdom movement.

I'd also say we need to give some discussion to *your 12*, your "group," before the discipleship journey we've taken with you in this workbook comes to a close. We talked so much about *your 1* in this workbook - that 1 person you've been a gospel-giver and disciple-maker too – and it's all been worth it just for that 1. I'm also going to trust you've connected yourself with a church (*your 120*) and that you're getting excited about being part of Jesus' kingdom movement (*your 3,000*). But it's that "grouping" of *your 12* in this gospel equation that I feel is loaded with so much gospel potential that needs to be realized.

Jesus spent a disproportionate amount of time with his group. It was *his 12* that got the extra layer of the lesson when everyone left. His 12 got out of town and away from the work to rest and pray at length. They got the extra challenges, the extra conversations, the extra discipleship - both with Jesus and with each other - *because they were grouped together.*

---

*Stop passing judgment on one another (Romans 14:3). Accept one another (Romans 15:7). Instruct one another (Romans 15:14). Greet one another (Romans 16:16). Agree with one another (1 Corinthians 1:10). Serve one another (Galatians 5:13). Be patient, bearing with one another (Ephesians 4:2). Be kind and compassionate to one another (Ephesians 4:32). Submit to one another (Ephesians 5:2). Teach and admonish one another (Colossians 3:16). And more if we didn't get tired of copying and pasting!*

---

Your friend needs your group. Just one on one with you (as amazing as I'm sure you are!) they are still not going to get a well-rounded picture of Jesus. Just going to church on Sunday, your friend might get lost in the crowd or settle for a spectator seat. In a group setting, however, your friend will be known, and experience belonging in the family of God and challenged all the more. They'll readily see that discipleship is hands-on growth and that they have something to offer. Invite them to church. Keep up your one-on-one relationship. But it is so important to form a group *around* them. Maybe, even go so far as to create a group *for* them.

## Workspace

If you're already "grouped" with others around Jesus, to what extent do you think your friend would mesh well there?

Even if you are already in a group, take this space to imagine what it might look like to create a group specifically around and for your friend.

1. Name anyone who's been a part of your discipleship discussions with your friend already.

2. Name some friends of your friend, who could be invited.

3. Name some Christian friends you love journeying with who could be invited.

4. When is an ideal time, and where is an ideal place to gather more regularly?

5. What is a common topic that would benefit everyone's discipleship?

6. What shared mission might you all engage in to bring more of Jesus' kingdom among us?

7. Who might lead this with you?

## Challenge

Start a group with your friends. If something already exists that's way too spot-on not to join, then join that. In many cases, though, God's ready to do new work with you, and you need to embrace that. You've got your new discipleship relationship with your friend, and I bet the two of you could name a handful of others who would want to group and gather around the kind of discipleship you share as well. Invite them. Pick a time, topic, and mission. See what happens.

# Extras

Grouping is what we do on *The Shape of a Circle* podcast! For creating a group and caring for an ongoing group, we've got a bunch of extras to leave you with.

## Starting Your Group

*31. Getting Started: Where to find people ready to be Discipled*

*32. Getting Started: Five Life Phases for Discipleship Settings*

*33. Getting Started: Ground Rules & Covenants*

*34. Getting Started: 5 Discussion Questions that Work Everywhere in the Bible*

*35. Getting Started with Discipleship Content*

*36. Getting Started with Mission for Your Community*

*37. Getting Started with a Multiplication Plan*

*38. Getting Start with Group Relationships*

## Ongoing Care for Your Group

# Epilogue

As others took the time to come alongside me (Cammie), invest in fully building a relationship with me (without a superficial agenda to get me into the door of their church or push their beliefs at me), I felt I could exhale. I felt I had been holding my breath my whole (Christian) life as I often wondered, "Is this it?"

I was so thankful that my mentors and friends didn't assume I was growing because I attended church and believed. I needed someone to ask, notice, and invite me into their lives to show me how to grow in Christ. I needed someone to walk the path WITH me, not merely give me directions.

Never assume your friend knows how.

Never assume they don't want it because they don't actively seek it.

You never know what a person's heart is muddling through and how God can use you to walk WITH them.

Want to know the cool part? It's when you experience growth ALONGSIDE your friend.

You're ready.

Go be a disciple who makes disciples in your everyday life.

Made in the USA
Monee, IL
13 January 2023

25244735R00069